Robert Schumann

COMPLETE SYMPHONIES

in Full Score

Robert Schumann

COMPLETE SYMPHONIES
in Full Score

From the Breitkopf & Härtel Complete Works Edition

EDITED BY CLARA SCHUMANN

Dover Publications, Inc.
New York

This Dover edition, first published in 1980, is an unabridged and unaltered republication of *Serie I. Symphonien für Orchester. Partitur* from *Robert Schumann's Werke. Herausgegeben von Clara Schumann,* originally published by Breitkopf & Härtel, Leipzig, as follows: Symphony No. 1, 1881; Symphonies No. 2 and No. 3, 1887; Symphony No. 4, 1882.

The table of contents and glossary of German terms are new features in the present edition.

The publisher is grateful to the Sibley Music Library of the Eastman School of Music, Rochester, N.Y., for making its material available for reproduction.

International Standard Book Number: 0-486-24013-4
Library of Congress Catalog Card Number: 80-66134

Manufactured in the United States of America
Dover Publications, Inc.
31 East 2nd Street, Mineola, N.Y. 11501

CONTENTS

GLOSSARY OF GERMAN TERMS IN SYMPHONIES NO. 3 AND NO. 4

As: A-flat
ausdrucksvoll: with expression
Des: D-flat
Die Halben wie vorher die Viertel: the half notes equal
    the preceding quarter notes
Etwas zurückhaltend: holding back somewhat
Feierlich: solemnly
H: B-natural
immer: continuing
immer schwächer und schwächer: becoming gradually
    quieter
Im Tempo: in tempo

Langsam: slowly
Lebhaft: vivaciously
markirt: marcato
Nach und nach stärker: louder little by little
Nicht schnell: not fast
Romanze: romance
Saite: string
Schneller: faster
sehr getragen: very sustained
Sehr mässig: very moderately
Ziemlich langsam: rather slowly

TRANSLATION OF FOOTNOTES

Page 72: To facilitate the ensemble playing in this passage, the conductor may
    give two beats before the beginning of the *Quasi Presto.*
Page 384: These *sf*, which are repeated later, must be produced by increasing
    breath power of the wind and brass players.

Symphony No. 1 in B-flat Major, Op. 38 ("Spring")

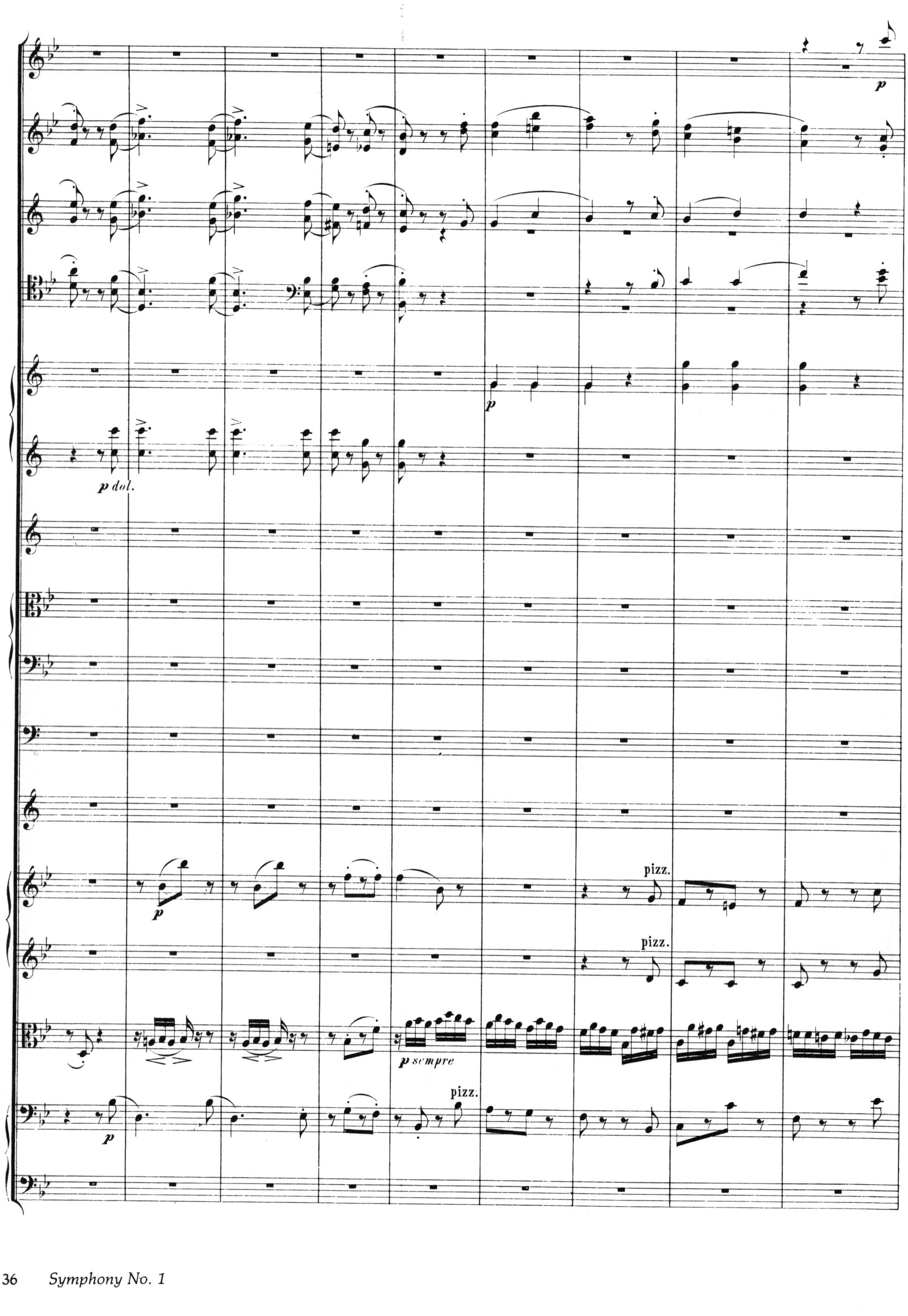
p
p dol.
p
pizz.
pizz.
p sempre
pizz.
p

Trio I.
Molto più vivace. ($\circ$ = 108.)

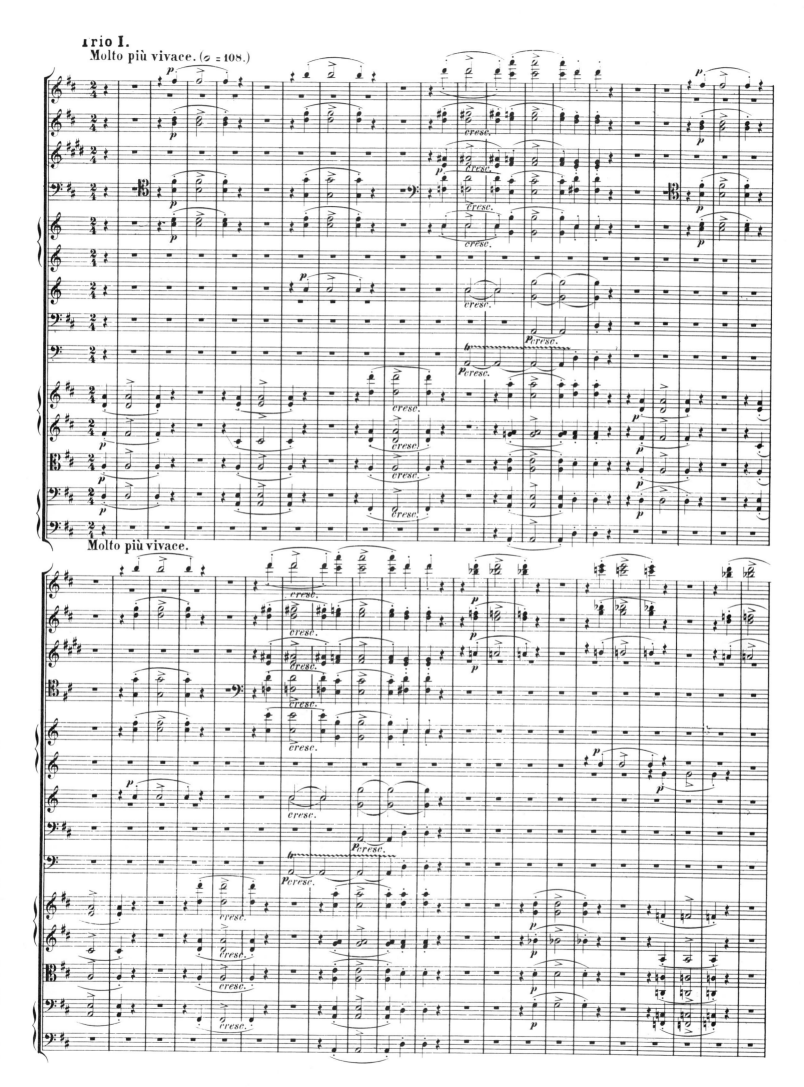

Molto più vivace.

Trio II.

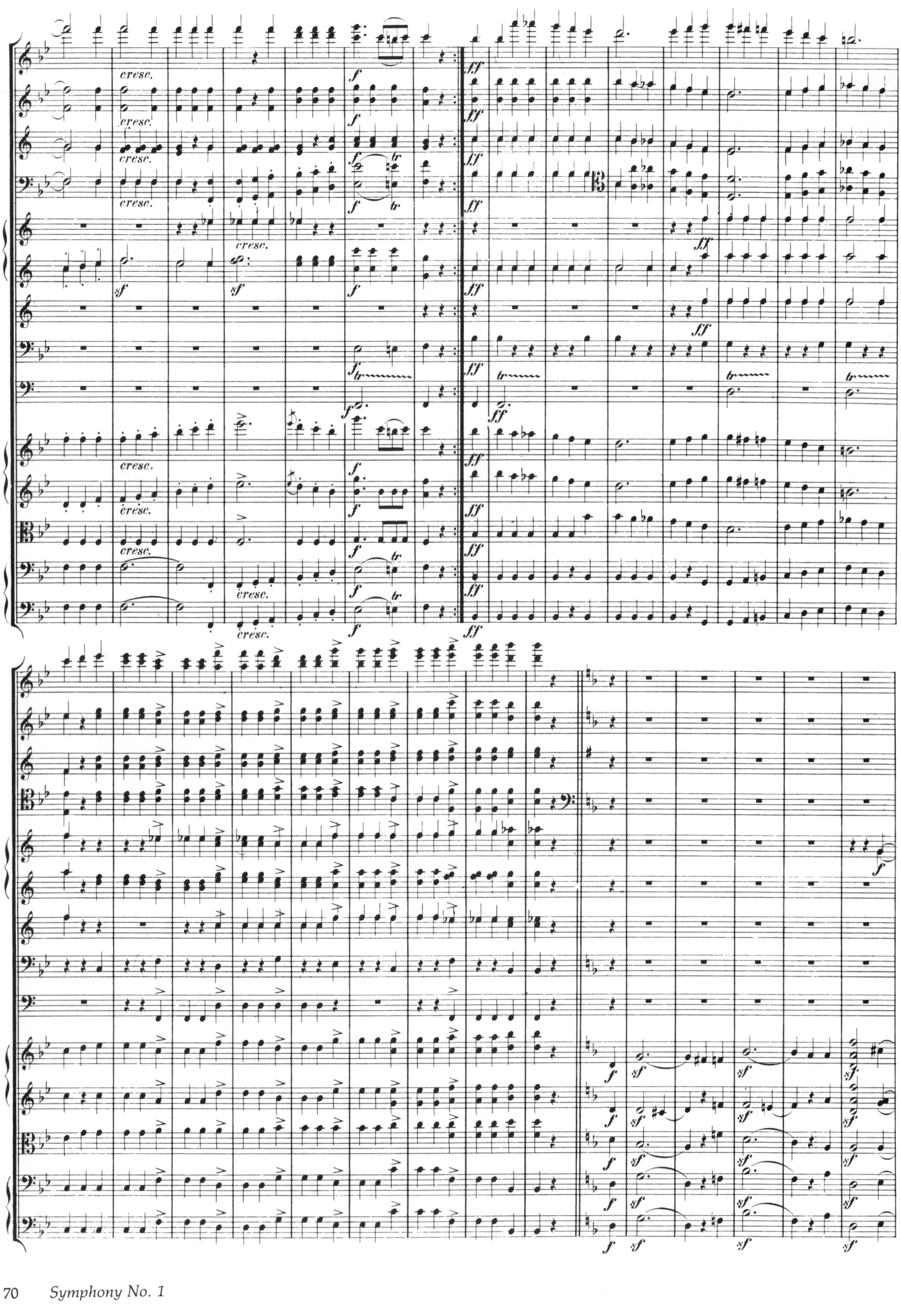
cresc.
f
ff
sf
tr

Coda.

Come sopra ma un poco più lento.

Quasi Presto.

ritard.

Come sopra ma un poco più lento.

ritard. — — — dim. Quasi Presto.

Meno Presto.

*) Zur Erleichterung des Zusammengehns dieser Stelle kann der Dirigent vor Anfang des Quasi Presto zwei Schläge angeben.

Meno Presto.

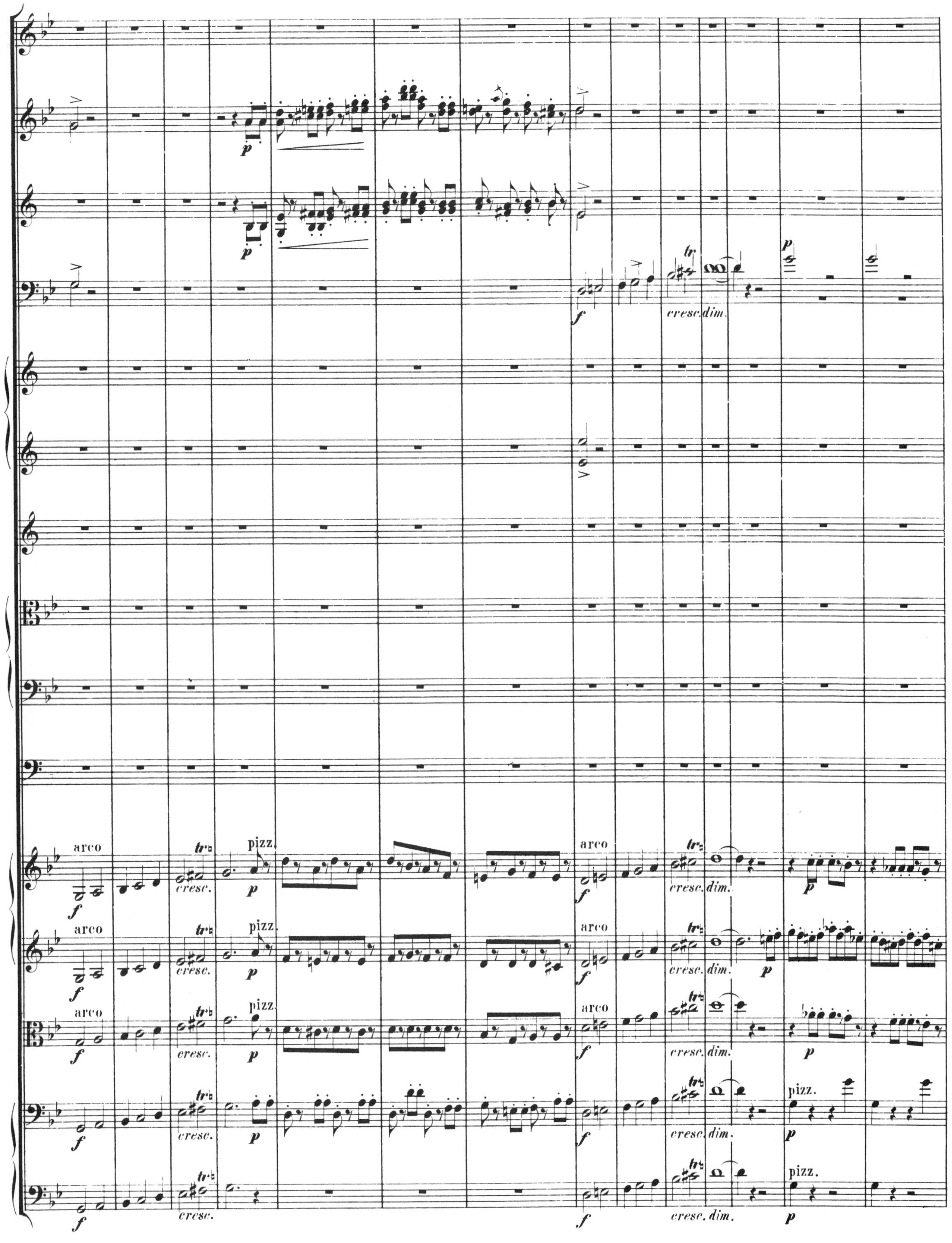
arco
pizz.
cresc.
dim.
arco
pizz.
cresc.
dim.
pizz.

p
I.
p
p
dim.
p
p
dim.
p
p
dim.
dim.
f
marcatiss.
f
marcatiss.
pp
pp
pizz.
div.
pp
pp
pizz.
div.
pp
pp
pizz.
pizz.
arco
pp
pizz.
pp
pp

Symphony No. 2 in C Major, Op. 61

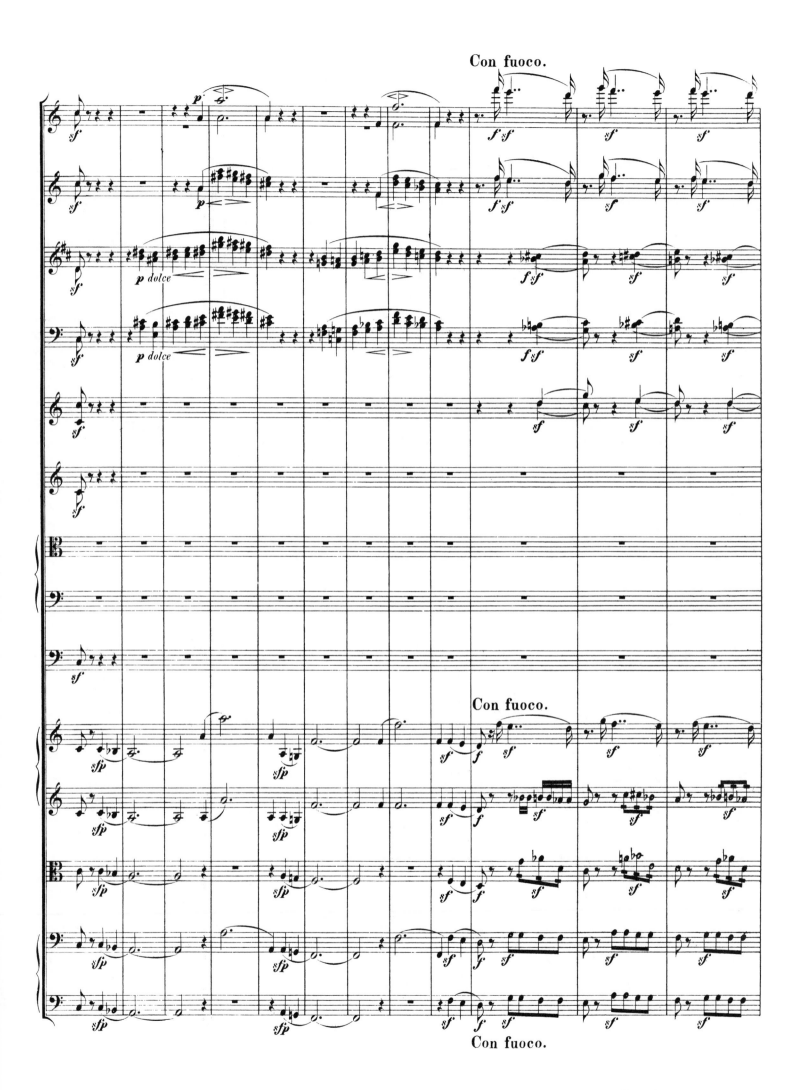

SCHERZO.

Allegro vivace. ♩= 144.

Flauti.

Oboi.

Clarinetti in B.

Fagotti.

Corni in C.

Trombe in C.

Timpani in C.G.

Violino I.

Violino II.

Viola.

Violoncello.

Basso.

Allegro vivace.

Trio I.

Trio II.

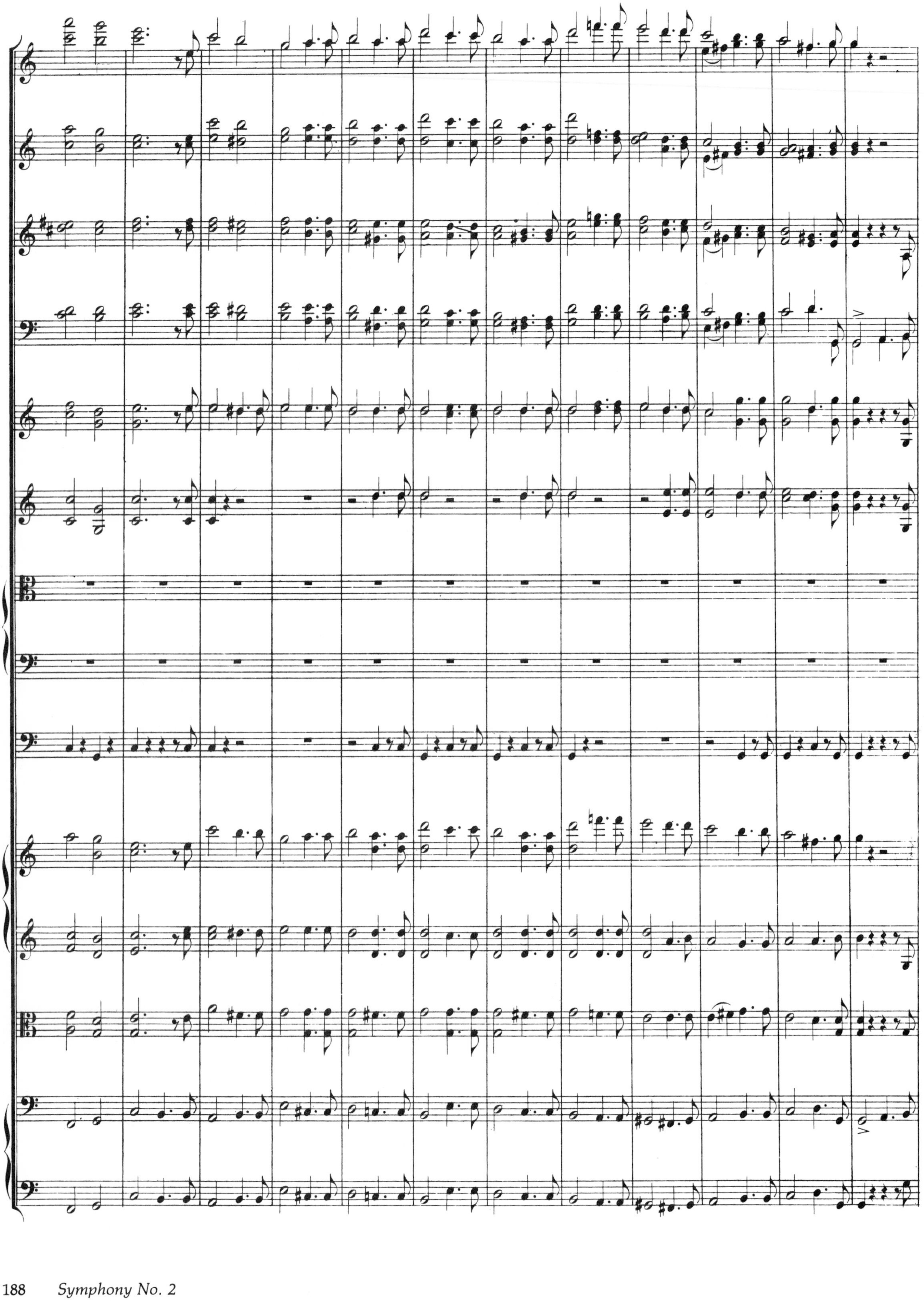

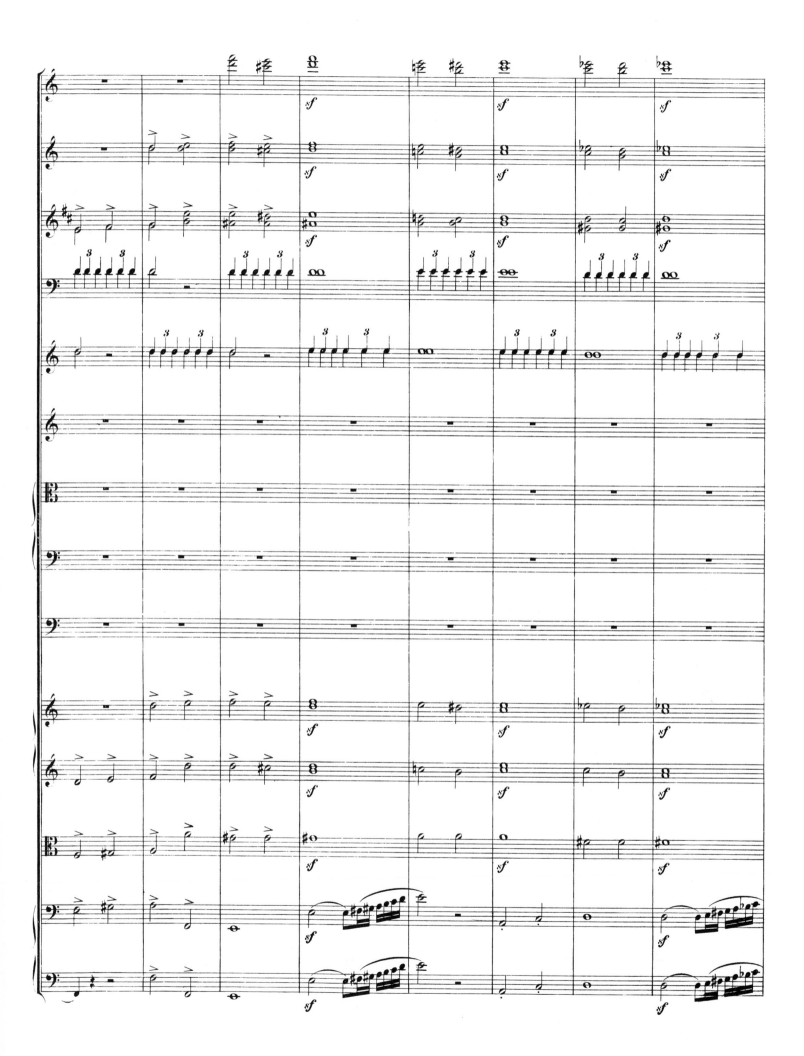

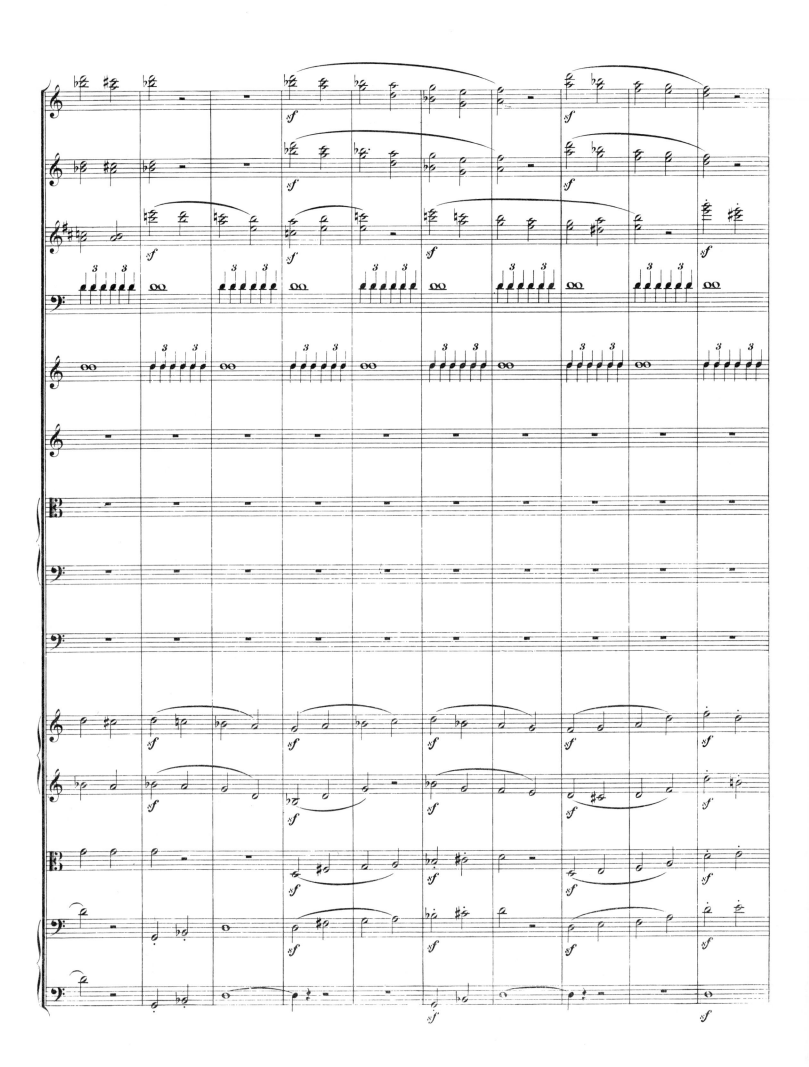

L'istesso tempo.

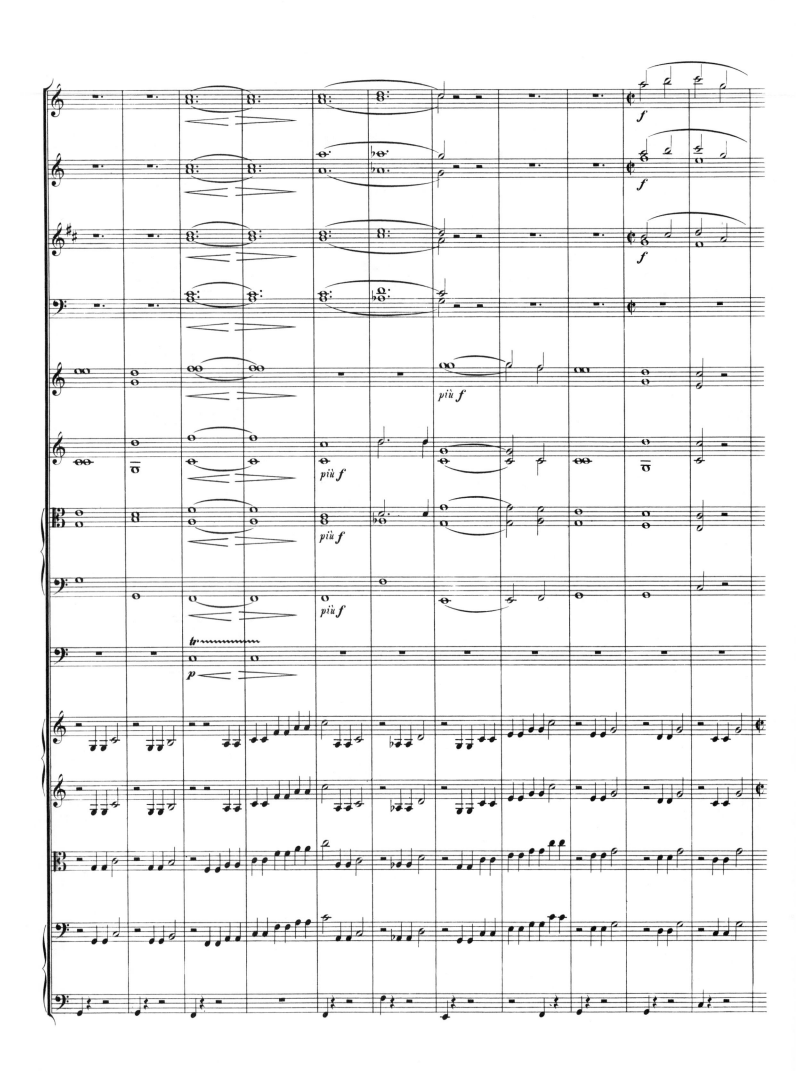

232   *Symphony No. 2*

Symphony No. 3 in E-flat Major, Op. 97 ("Rhenish")

I.

SCHERZO.

II.

Sehr mässig. ♩ = 100.

Flauti.

Oboi.

Clarinetti in B.

Fagotti.

Corni in F.

Corni in C.

Trombe in F.

Timpani in C. G.

Violino I.

Violino II.

Viola.

Violoncello.

Basso.

III.

IV.

Symphony No. 4 in D Minor, Op. 120

Die Skizze dieser Symphonie entstand bereits im Jahre 1841 kurz nach der Ersten in B dur, wurde aber erst im Jahre 1851 vollständig instrumentirt. Diese Bemerkung schien nöthig, da später noch zwei mit den Nummern II und III bezeichnete Symphonien erschienen sind, die, der Zahl der Entstehung nach, folglich die III te und IV te wären.

muta in Des. As.

in Des As.

ROMANZE.

Fl. **Ziemlich langsam.** ($\text{♩} = 66.$)

Ziemlich langsam.

Ziemlich langsam.

SCHERZO.
Lebhaft. (♩ = 92.)

Etwas zurückhaltend.

*) Diese, später wiederholte *sf* müssen von den Blasinstrumentalisten durch wachsende Kraft der Brust hervorgebracht werden.